ASPIRATIONS AND FULFILMENT

Taimur Awan
Aspirations and Fulfilment

Published by BooxAI
ISBN: 978-965-578-616-3

ASPIRATIONS AND FULFILMENT

TAIMUR AWAN

CONTENTS

PREFACE

When an author or poet ventures into the vast field of literature his main enterprise is to define the human condition. My first collection of poems is the fruit of my studies in Greek and Islamic philosophy. I wish to define and clarify certain universal topics such as faith, falling in love, lust, and the divine beauty of the natural world and our connection with God. To connect with a wider audience, I have avoided Shakespearean and Miltonic diction and chosen simpler words. I am aware that this collection is not all inclusive in its scope and a second collection is on its way.

Best Wishes

Taimur Awan

London, 9 September. 2023

Aspirations and Fulfilment

Many consider worldly life

To be an episode of suffering,

A prison and jail,

We aspire to the skies,

For the fulfilment of our dreams aspirations,

And desires,

Yet like an eagles cut wings,

Are bound to the level sahara.

God, allow me entrance to the flowery meadows,

Vast expanses, and like a falcon soar,

Above all the summits of humanity,

Become an oasis to quench my thirst,

Be the fulfiller of all my desires.

Poets

Poets are beauticians, embellishers, and aestheticians,

Providing the regal banquets of philosophy, psychology, theology,

I am not addicted to life's dark realities,

But the light, colour, and fragrance of existence,

A torch can kindle many candles,

Let my poetry be like a congregation of violets,

Spreading perfumes east and west,

Till I achieve laurels, crowns, and victories.

Healing

Dear God, remove pain and fire from my heart,

Heal the injuries of my heart, body, and mind,

Till I enjoy the endless fountains of happiness.

A single Star

Out of all the galaxies of beautiful women

I am in search of a solitary star

The light of my heart the jewel of my lifetime

Because a woman with a beautiful body

Pure heart and intellectual mind

Is a gift from God and will be the princess of my mortality.

Glimpses of God

Divine and alien sunsets,

That rest on the mirror of calm oceans,

Their rays filling the horizon with rays of beauty,

Are a glimpse of god.

Perfection Achieved

We must fall many times before we learn to walk endlessly,

We must sin countless times before we achieve the summit of piety,

Hearts polished like gold, syllables and actions of righteousness,

With fortified and lifelong faith in God,

when the light of the universe shines upon our hearts,

Like a lamp kindled by a flame that burns for a lifetime,

Till pain, fire, and lust is removed from our lives forever.

Unrequited Passion

Beauties have cast their arrows of fire in my heart,

By me falling in love a thousand times, they as distant as the stars,

Why should fire and pain consume my heart,

Or lust be the existential plague, canceler of spirituality,

When I possess the royalties of faith and virtue,

Which are the keys to the gates of eternal paradise,

I know the most beautiful princess of humanity will be my reward.

On Falling in Love

Falling in love is madness intoxication and endless obsession,

He behaves like a drunkard and she becomes his never ending pursuit,

She becomes like a drug with fatal withdrawal symptoms,

So why create idols out of beauties, or become idolators,

When god should be our timeless orbit?

Burn me Lord

Burn me lord in the fiercest of fires your alchemy upon me bestow,

Like pure gold from the over darkened chaff,

Like a phoenix blessed by newer life,

Like a furnace transforms coal to gold,

The fires of tribulations transform our personalities,

Then grant me the very summit of piety,

That tower above Sinai, above the Alps,

A lifetime adorned with faith, charity, and good acts,

A heart of polished gold, the zenith of sainthood,

Till you become for my thirst, an all quenching oasis,

Like drinking from the fountains of universal knowledge,

Till humanity is before me like an open scroll,

All her secrets and realities revealed.

A Tribute to Keats

In tubercular entrails he hymned to beauty,

Of poesy's sky aspiring wings,

That will everlastingly enchant posterity,

Like the briar at the breast of the nightingale,

The most over sweetened soul ever to have existed,

Yet he was victim to the scourges of cruel analysis,

Yet he now rests in the most gorgeous of Elysium's,

Eagerly witnessing his universal fame,

The fruits and blossoms of prodigious labour,

Enjoying his eternal health and felicity divine,

The incense and perfume he bestowed to generations.

On her Blindness

Blindness veiled her from the lovely cradle of sunrise,

When the sun's rays illuminate the oceans and the lakes,

From the meadows, gardens, and flowers, and incense groves,

From snowlike faces and honeyed societies,

From divine sunsets resting on the mirror of tranquil oceans,

Her history will be a blank page in the chronicles of poets,

Yet my verses will spread the fragrance of her memory east and west,

Like a Nargis blossom to fill all future generations with perfumes.

Obstacles to Victory in Life

Often persons and circumstances are our enemies,

The walls and obstacles on our route to success,

Faith in god and purity of heart breaks walls,

Demolishes and defeats all obstacles,

And grants us success and trophies.

Wreckage

Out of all the wreckage and ruin of their lives,

The alpha of faith in God has birth,

They are reborn and build new empires,

Adorned with worship, charity, and loving actions,

With golden qualities that reach the summits of piety,

They forget the injuries of their antiquity,

And enjoy the orient and sunrise of a new life,

With the injuries of their hearts, bodies, and minds healed,

Their worship and annual prayers bear fruit,

With flowers in their mortality, and gorgeous blossoms in post-eternity.

Questers for God

The questers for God journey east, west, north, and south,

To Byzantium, Rome, Persia, and Greece,

To all antiquity and all futurity,

The evergreen and fertile and pastoral regions of earth,

By the mere caravan of their imagination,

And their vision pierces the divine world,

And they witness the alien universe of eternity.

An Elegy for my Cousin Saba

Snatched forever, like the fresh berries of the spring,

By the theft of baskets to the vast wilderness,

Was your pure and divine soul, now custodian of death,

From virginities lovely prime to the ever silent cemetery,

Heaped with garlands and only a memorial stone,

Begin then, refreshing fountains of hippocrene,

To fill my goblet with mixtures of wine divine,

That divine inspiration forces me to write,

Poetry matchless in the pantheons of posterity,

Like the emblazoned orb of the beaming sun,

Decorates the mountain tops with rays of glory,

Kisses the oceans and lakes with hues of serenity,

Blesses the roses, tulips, and violets,

With gentle caressing, and quivering breezes,

That their combined perfumes delight the Grecian pastorals,

Attired in garments of Phoenician silk,

Your triumphant soul shall enter the gates of eternal paradise.

Lamentations of the Muse

When the muse beckons, like the chant of the muezzin for prayers,

A single torch can kindle a thousand candles,

Not extinguished by the gusts and breezes of a lifetime,

And fill manuscripts with syllables of supreme beauty,

That become the enchantment and perfume of generations,

Like the sun's orb upon the cimmerian midnight,

With divine rays fills the horizon with glory,

And the serene mirror of lakes with lovely hues,

Awakens the slumbering larks with choirs,

I lament upon dido's lovesick quest for Aeneas,

Her blazing pyre, consuming her gorgeous anatomy,

Or odysseus, with labouring ships beyond the horizons boundary,

Or socrates, accepting the goblet of hemlock, lamenting youths,

Like moths encircling an expiring flame,

I celebrate atlas, bearing the load of the constellations,

The whirling orbits and planets,

Or the seven herculean labours,

Of sinews of steel vanquishing wild beasts and lions,

Or ebony cleopatra, snake coiling around her, hissing with aspic,

And draining her of her sinful life.

On Mortality

Mortality is like a mountain steep,

And each quest and fiery ambition be,

A falcons clipped wings desiring the loftiest sky,

Yet I am content sailing on the tranquil waves,

Or level plains with breeze quivering daffodils,

And seek not the legendary Sinai's that tower,

Yet the cruel genocide of life's treasuries I lament,

Like temples destroyed, or locusts upon harvests.

On Worldly Life

Worldly life is a void and a zero,

Futile, profitless, an abyss of pain,

We quest for the fulfilment of our desires, dreams, and aspirations,

Like goals to reach fulfilment,

Like archery to hit their targets,

Yet cancelled by the shears of destiny,

I would rather barter this futile life,

For the boundless ocean of eternity,

Of everlasting felicity, beauty, love, and health,

Beyond sight and hearing, the visionary mind,

The veiled future that awaits the righteous,

When the curtains and veils are lifted off eternal life.

A Love Song

Falling in love is the genesis of life's happiness,

The light of feeling, the perfume of feeling,

Yet a cliff, and a precipice,

Love is as constant as the northern star,

Lovers are like two twin roses,

The union of bodies, hearts, and minds for a lifetime,

May not the trials and tribulations of existence,

Like a knife cut the rope of that blessed union

She is the east, dawn, and sunrise of my life,

She forever erases the eclipses of my antiquity

Her beauty is the light and perfume of my heart,

She is the jewel of my lifetime,

May times chariot speed me thru midnights wilderness,

To the morn of our lifelong union,

I swear by the eternal jewelries of the stars,

Whose cruel dictatorships we shall never obey,

That we are the captains that steer our ships courses,

Thru seas of winds, storms, and tempests,

And our sacred romance shall be registered,

In all the everlasting annals of humanity.

Signs of God

Divine and alien sunsets,

That rest on the mirror of calm oceans,

Their rays filling the horizon with beauty,

Are a glimpse of God,

So are starlit domes and moonlit oceans,

And flowery gardens,

And paradisal twilights,

In all the glory and majesty of the infinite universe,

Are the signs and signatures of God.

Love Poems

Thousands of stone hearted beauties have cast their arrows of fire in my heart,

By the intensity of my love and their hearts like brass or lifeless glaciers,

Distant and indifferent as the blazing constellations,

Because of their beauty and their charms,

Or their physical displays, unveiled and nude,

Dear God, the beauties of the globe are my torment,

Why did you create such seducing populations,

To divert righteous men from the path of light and piety?

Answer not this distress of lust with your universal silence,

But the marriage to the princess of my fantasies,

Her body, a sacred gift to my lifetime,

There are beauties in the millions, like stars in galaxies,

Grant me a single star, and she will fill me with the light of life,

Beautiful women are the gifts, quests, trophies,

The gravities of endless lust and desire,

Cancel eros, and let agape claim the sceptre.

Eros and Nature

Princess, like you, having no desire,

For male Greek gods, or Hercules bare,

Females have little or low degrees of lust,

Intellect, generosity, and kindness,

Are outshining qualities they seek in men,

Your bare form once pierced me with arrows of lust,

Plagued with wild hounds,

Now I glance not at beauties,

Stark naked on stage, or bikinis by poolside,

I divert and lower my gaze,

At divine sunsets, or moon illuminated midnights,

Shining on the mirror of tranquil oceans,

I have no more desire or lust for beauties,

The exit door is open, freeze in the zeros,

I am warm by my fire side.

Greek Goddess

Greek goddess, flaunting her bare body,

Dress yourself in a veil or hijab,

Face whiter than the moon, wild blonde tresses,

You congregations of perfect sculpted beauties,

You do not impress me you cast no lustful arrows,

I am protected by the shield of faith,

Excellence in words and syllables,

Excellence in actions, perfections in conduct,

Are all herculean qualities,

God is the lifelong orbit of my life,

Who will gift me with a beauty,

Outshining all the stars of females,

A treasury of beauty, wisdom, and a golden heart.

Predestiny

Whatever I feel and experience in life,

Is but God's design and his decree,

My before written, pre-ordained biography,

Why should I fear cyclopean Vicissitudes,

Or the fathomless Gehenna's of suffering,

When they are but signs and signets,

Of God's wisdom, and of his art,

How victorious my soul shall stand,

Before the gates of everlasting paradise.

On Contentment

What would you prefer,

The zeros of Russia or the scorching Sahara?

I would prefer the warm fields of Tuscany,

In winter we complain in frost, in summer of heat,

Faith in God is the light of the heart, body, and mind.

On Pious Women

Pious women make a caricature of Greek goddesses,

Helen of troy struggling with the aeolian lyre,

Sent to be tutored at the academies of Athens,

Bare female anatomies, the instruments of Satan,

Of Aphrodite, Venus, without garments or apparel,

Or fierce amazons defeating squadrons after squadrons
of sinewy warriors,

Leaving battlefields of groaning and dying men,

Where over a darkened nook above,

An exultant nightingale sings her song,

Why should eros raise her sceptre?

Her banner of victory over my pious life,

Dedicated to God like a timeless orbit,

When only spiritual nectars I can relish?

Our Secret Romance

Nikki, do you remember when our romance,

Was a safe sanctuary against the arrows of this cold and indifferent humanity?

Surrounded by gorgeous and serene expanses,

Seated beneath the cypress tree,

Under the canopy of moonlit and starlit skies,

Shining on midnight lakes,

Holding hands and uttering syllables of beauty,

Those memories of far antiquity have fragrances and a thorn.

On Lust

David's lust for Bathsheba,

Amnon's for his half-sister,

One lost his kingdom,

The other his dignity,

The lineage of imperial bloods debased to bestiality,

Did not fair Joseph flee the invitation to Zulaikha's bed?

Delilah and Sheba, false seductresses, I flee,

But seek Zipphhora, Ruth, or Aiesha,

Whom seraphic scribes, in the annals of history praised.

On True Love

Lovers are like two twin roses,

Love is as constant as the northern star,

The union of bodies, hearts, and minds for a lifetime,

The henna on a beautiful brides hands,

Cannot be removed for her entire mortality,

Like waves upon waves of generations upon the everlasting shore,

Time cannot erase their love signatures.

On the Poet

The poet is the healer, fragrance, and delight of posterity,

By a quill and parchment, the conquest of humanity,

He fears not the fierce militancy's of time,

Being a symbol of the divine,

Giving birth to the monarchies of verse,

To all the thorn filled and poisoned hearts,

He grants all the floods of felicity,

The orphic balm, the wizardry of syllables,

Come Helen, destroyer of troy,

Come Sophia and Aphrodite,

Come Minerva, invincible lioness,

Deflect the spears that stone hearted beauties,

Fling upon my purified heart,

A poet's empire is never destroyed,

Yet fills with perfumes all future generations,

Like violet blossoms spreading perfumes east and west,

Let the falconry of my verse soar above all the summits of posterity.

Her Priceless Love

Were I to possess the crown of virtue,

I would barter them all for her priceless love,

The victory, conquest, and coronation of my life,

Or a beggar, seeker, quester for a lifetime,

Her face is whiter than the full moon,

Her lips and cheeks of ruby, lustrous black tresses,

Her body, a masterpiece of creation,

The nectar of her mouth,

Fragrances of fresh musk from her body,

What profits the tyrant in his ruthless decrees,

The sceptre that bears the signet of falsehood,

When my all-consuming love,

Is worth more than the burnings and bloodshed of multitudes,

The choiring larks that herald the golden dawn,

The sun's rays that beautify oceans and lakes,

The legions of floras that fill the meadows with incense,

None is like the fragrance of her gentle affections.

Thirst Satisfied

She will be the lasting fountain for my thirst,

My glass is empty,

Her affections are worth more than a thousand intoxicating goblets of wine,

I have been filled with pizzas and pastas,

My appetite satisfied,

Her love will be the banquet and feast of my life,

When my hunger and thirst for love and romance is fulfilled,

Like a falcon, I will soar above the summits of happiness.

On the Purpose of Life

Earthquakes, volcanoes, floods, cyclones,

The disasters and calamities upon multitudes,

Mutilations, dagger wounds, burnings, bloodshed.

Injuries and all fatal diseases,

Warfare, poverty, endless crusades,

The holocaust of the Jews,

The terror of the Mongol armies,

The infinite atrocities in the annals of history,

My faith in God is not questioned,

But the curse of birth,

The genesis of civilization,

Yet the genesis of civilization is a gift,

The precipice and cliff of falling in love,

Of romances sweet, gazing on divine sunsets,

Of excellent women, gifted with beauty, charms, and wisdom,

Of universities, academies, and sacred scriptures,

That instruct elevate, and illuminate humanity,

Of moonlit domes and starlit oceans,

That speak the language of divinity,

Of picturesque gardens at paradisal twilights,

Of passing the difficulties, injuries, and afflictions of life,

With lifelong and fortified faith in God.

Mars vs Venus

Mars is at war with Venus,

who wins?

Men are not superior to women,

Both genders are equal morally and intellectually,

Women deserve more careers,

And ivy league degrees,

They hold the crown and sceptre of loftier qualities,

Even mars or Ares would lay down their swords,

If Venus or Aphrodite proposed with a bouquet of floras.

Religious Poems

God's empire extends beyond the universe,

Our planet but a speck of dust in the limitless cosmos,

Supremist of all wisdoms,

Instruct me in the infancy of my wisdom,

Make my personality into a monument of excellence,

Defined as the sapphire union of firmament and ocean,

Make my life's quest for you an all-quenching oasis,

My thirsty being for the fulfilment of all my desires,

Till humanity is before me like an open scroll,

All her secrets and realities revealed.

On Free Will

Would fiery Zeus, throned on the top of Olympus,

If given choice and free will,

To destroy the fertile and green expanses of Athens,

Or to let them flourish for a utopian immortality,

He would strike fiery and sulphur bolts,

And destroy temples, populations, and nations,

A saint or a prophet is born to save and redeem populations,

Free will is either a sword or a healing balm.

Faith's Universal Beacon

Not Aphrodite, Venus, or painted Helen,

Or all the myriads of Grecian beauties,

Cast their arrows of lust,

I am protected by a shield of bronze,

I seek not the wisdom of Plato, Socrates, or Seneca,

Or astrology, prophecy, Delphic oracles, all falsified arts,

Like a thirsty and wandering pilgrim I seek the Kaaba's shrine,

I seek the Koran universal beacon of light,

The lantern for my darkest path.

Love and Lust

Love and lust are not the same,

We feel love for our parents and pets,

We feel love for doves and fragrant roses,

Yet do not desire to have throbbing's with them in bed,

Lust is physical desire for nude Venus, or bare Aphrodite,

With no degree of affection for the desired object,

Such are the fair fleshed beauties in secret harems,

They are perfumed, polished, and bred for sexual delight,

The sultan has no affection for them, only cruelty and subjugation.

On Reading the Persian Poets

Standing aloof in gigantic felicity,

Like having drunk a thousand goblets of wine,

Admiring of moon white faces of Houries,

With rose red lips and cheeks

And bodies that are more perfect than Greek sculptures

Touched by the priceless ornaments of verse,

I climb a mountain top,

And at the zenith witnessed the majesty of Shiraz.

My Refuge

Amorous of nature's paradisal masterworks,

Inventions of providence,

A diviner sacrament in me is born,

Defying the eclipses multitudes of humanity,

To find Eden in Grasmere's tributaries,

Opium filled meditations,

And golden solitudes,

And amid these ageless floras,

Where time writes no wrinkle or decay,

I have no need for creed or scripture,

Like those balmy delphic prophecies,

I seek the palms of a diviner life,

And as my life's ebbing dynasty fades,

I seek salvation, and the alien universe of eternal life.

A prayer

Lord, cancel my sins like a white garment is cleansed of dark stains,

Like a lilac garden, by the scythe of the gardener is purged of weeds,

Let the flame of love and virtue burn constantly in my heart,

Remove me from all iniquity like the sky is removed from the ground,

Let not legions of vultures and cormorants prey on the safe sanctuary of my being.

Her Beauty

Her beauty is like the sun's burning torch,

From aloft her meridian station in the sky,

Gives light to my heart, and burns my heart to ashes,

She is like the gift of the east, a fresh sunrise,

May her beauty never decline into the mournful apparel of the west,

Though oceans part us, and nations divide us,

Times chariot will speed me to our lifelong union,

Her sculpted beauty, excelling all Phidian masterworks,

Her throb causing image, and lifegiving zones,

Her visage, painted in full white and pink,

Is like the moons shining lamp,

Hung above the gloomy midnight.

On Maturity

The faults we see in others are our own faults,

Polish the mirror, saint and sinner stand the same,

Black and white are reflected in the glass,

Pharaoh or Genghis Khan,

Emblems of fire and eclipses,

Or Jesus and Mustafa,

Paragons of light,

Are the produce of the same world,

Our wisdom is like an embryo,

Before the supremist of all wisdoms,

The lord of the universe has bestowed a sun,

That our infant seed may ripen into maturity.

On Marriage

A woman might appear to be beautiful,

A visage fair as the full moon, well sculpted in body,

Yet her heart can contain fires and eclipses,

If a man weds her for her beauty,

And cannot see beyond the veil,

He is breeding a serpent,

A diver in the ocean is in search for priceless pearls,

True love is a unique treasure, barter it not for trash,

A woman with beauty and a pure heart,

An angel in utterances and actions,

Is the peak of virtues,

Loftiest in creations hierarchy,

An exhaustless fountain of happiness for her husband,

His thirst forever quenched.

My Desires into Reality

The king has the power to imprison, execute, or consign to the gallows,

The fiery tyrant is the genocide of millions,

Celebrate, for the king of kings has kindled a light in my heart,

Given me hopes of moon white faces of houris, with pink lips and cheeks,

That like Alexander, I will conquer one,

My endless fountain of wine, goblets served endlessly

A bride with a supreme body, intellect, and golden heart,

The response to my faith, rosaries, and lifelong prayers

See how the chariot of time will speed me to my delight.

A Prayer for Excellence

Lord, let my embryonic intellect mature into a sages wisdom,

Let the seed of my peace flower into felicity supreme,

Let me follow the ever-spinning courses of the planets,

Like the timeless orbit, my faith in God,

Let my faith, like a fierce sword,

Slay vicissitudes like a battlefield filled with centaurs,

The final, flying banner of victory,

My life, the gift of Capricorn,

To bear fealty with the constellations,

Till with your divine aid and miracle I win,

My prize, the most gorgeous princess in humanity,

Remove from my personality,

The stains of malice, pride, and arrogance,

And quench with monsoon showers,

The fires of hatred, anger, and jealousy,

Till I wander in heavenly pastures and meadows,

And lying beside crystalline streams.

On Solitude

From the crowded bazaars of the world,

I sought the sanctuary of solitude,

Lit by candles, incense, and meditation,

The light of creation filled my inner being,

I felt no relationship with humanity or the world,

That cast their fiery arrows and shafts in my heart,

But to the king of the universe,

The divine sunset and the glowing twilight,

The full moon reflected upon the waves of the midnight beach,

Gave me a glimpse into divinity.

On Falling in Love and Divine Beauty

Falling in love is the genesis of life's happiness,

And romance an era of excitement and pure delight,

Yet she becomes his addiction, obsession, and intoxication,

As if he is a drunkard,

She becomes like drug addiction with fatal withdrawal symptoms,

Without her, he is full of misery,

She becomes his idol worship, he forgets God,

He stands on the verge of a dangerous cliff and precipice,

Why should I create idols out of beauties,

When God is my timeless orbit?

Why should fiery Hera be my quest,

Or foul Hecate cast magic spells on my anatomy?

Her beauty is like the sunrise, and lasting fountains of Abe-zamzam,

That when I bathe in them, I am purified of the germs of life,

Purged of fire and eclipses, of all sin and iniquity,

Her beauty is like a rose-garden that blossoms for a lifetime,

Minus cankers, and never withered by the wintry snows,

Her love converts the poison of my heart into honey,

She is the divine female, a drop of light from the ocean of light.

On Faith

Fain in God is like the dawning sun,

It fills with light the hearts of its embracers,

Like the rays of the meridian sun nourishes the floras,

And gives life to the natural world and all its myriad flowerings,

It cancels existentialism and the quest for life's meaning and purpose,

It slays atheism with its universal sword,

And the puzzles of physicists,

It proves that God is the creator of the infinite cosmos,

It kindles the heart with an ever-burning flame,

That shines thru hardships, afflictions, injuries, and predicaments,

It is constantly at zenith, and knows no declining west,

We are purified in heart, gain the peaks of virtues,

Become paragons of excellence,

With control over the heart's fires.

We are showered with the everlasting fountains,

Cleansed from the germs of existence,

Even if our hopes and dreams seem like a mirage,

We discover an oasis.

My Life Fulfilled

I quest for marriage and fame like twin felicities,

Metaphors of victory over all my defeats in life,

For the falconry of my verses to soar to the stars,

For the prize of a woman with a beautiful body,

A golden heart and the loftiest wisdom,

These fulfilled will be the everlasting fountains for my thirst,

Confirmations of my faith in God,

Like two trophies hung amid the zodiacs,

I fall in love daily with gorgeous princesses,

Their unveiled anatomies casting the gravities of endless lust,

Yet their personalities are hieroglyphs and crypts,

The quest futile, till I discover the princess of my mortality,

The gift of God, Capricorn, and predestiny,

Like the full moon shining upon our divine romance,

Like Laila's lovely face, resembling white lilies and blushing roses,

She, appearing into my life from the hidden chambers of the east, the alpha and rebirth of my life.

A prayer for Light

God, bathe me in your refreshing fountains,

Like I shower daily, cleanse my heart and personality,

Of all the germs and infections of life,

Light of the universe, bestow upon my soul,

A drop of your light,

Till I become a symbol for future generations.

Philosophical Musings

Is a feast or regal banquet necessary?

Many are content with pitchers of milk And loaves of bread,

Multitudes quest after and achieve wealth,

Lofty status and political offices,

The very stamps of sovereignty,

Yet their hearts contain neither tranquillity nor light,

The palaces of Versailles, with flowing fountains and lush gardens,

Are the entrances and exits of arrogant monarchs and queens,

Yet who smuggled wealth into the tomb or dark sepulchre,

Save decaying anatomies?

A billionaire lying sick in his mansion,

Attended by maids and servants,

Is the very paragon of misery

I seek the face and anatomy of Sophia,

Her companionship and bond,

Her counsels and oratories of lofty wisdom,

And the painted, moon-white visage of Helen,

Deformed by ages all darkening acrylics,

Health and happiness are the light, colour, and perfume of life,

Inner and outer dungeons purged,

The radiance of the heart and the world,

Of evergreen expanses, and flowery realms,

Of full moons that shine on midnight oceans,

Of me and my princess, my quest and victory,

Our divine romance beneath moonlit lakes,

Of Laila's face resembling whitest Lillie's and blushing roses,

Appearing into my life from the hidden chambers of the east,

Like an alpha and rebirth of my existence,

Of Africa's ebony beauties scorched by the Libyan sun,

In their mirthful dances and festivals,

With Dionysus offering me many goblets of wine,

With my felicity reaching its zenith,

Or Orpheus playing the lyre, Aphrodite the flute,

Whose harmonious melodies fill the Grecian pastorals,

What greater paradise or Elysium on earth?

On Light

God is light, and God is eternal,

Without beginning, without end,

Progenitor of this limitless cosmos,

We, seated upon earth, this grain of sand,

Speculating on the interstellar beatitude,

Reflecting on the incomprehensible and fathomless,

God, you exist far, far, beyond the universes,

They cannot contain you, yet my finite, throbbing heart,

That overflows with love for you, is your lodging,

There are a few stars in the dark sky,

Who are your chosen, beloved, and elect,

Whom you guide with your universal beacon,

To the boundless paradise of eternity.

Secular Salvation

Futile are all the religions and creeds,

Like the faded roses in the winter,

To those who are the summits of virtues,

And keep the flame of love burning in their hearts.

The Faithful Believer

God is the creator of the twin orbs,

The burning torch that nourishes the earth,

The white lamp of the moon, that beautifies the silent midnight,

The faithful believers heart receives the light of the universe,

A flame kindled for a lifetime,

He is patient in calamity, by prayers and rosaries,

He answers not the calls of lust,

Controls his inner volcanoes,

Answers not arrow with arrow, or fire with fire,

All the highway robbers fail to ambush him,

Even if they steal his purse and commodities,

they can never steal his primal merchandise, faith

O salvation, and the boundless paradise of eternity.

My Salvation

I have endured the neglect and arrows of humanity,

Like shafts of fire cast in my heart by princesses,

What is a beautiful woman's face but a decaying flower,

Faded in its autumn, and decayed in winter,

Like a waning full moon,

What is mortality but the blink of an eye,

A brief second,

What is the light, colour, and fragrance of life,

When entombed in the black depth of the grave?

Why not sustain faith in God,

Be a billionaire in righteous deeds,

why not barter this life for the boundless paradise?

I love beauties like a bee is attracted to flowers,

Their affections more intoxicating than a thousand goblets of wine,

So let my mortality be a symbol of self-sacrifice,

For the victorious entrance into the gates of eternal paradise,

The quest for salvation

If our mortality is so temporary,

Why waste it in futile quests?

Like amassing wealth, and luxurious lifestyles,

When bestowing annual nourishment for the poor,

Are like a seed with a thousand grains of corn for us,

Without health, wealth is a broken equation,

So why not erase fire and eclipses from our personalities,

And germs from our hearts, by bathing in god's refreshing showers?

If faith in God, and purified hearts, The summits of perfection in piety,

The flame of love and goodness in the heart,

That burns naturally for a lifetime, is victory supreme,

The very charter for salvation, o gatekeeper,

Open your gates for the thirsty and weary pilgrims,

For caravans that can hear your distant celebrations and melodies,

Never a mirage, but an eternal oasis,

Are the sloping ridges of antique Arafat,

Where Adam received the bequest of repentance,

Be compensation for the abortive seed of humanity?

Is not crime, sin, oppression, cruelty, and injustice,

A rotten harvest that deserves the scythe and fire of the harvester?

To heal the cries of Kashmir and Palestine,

Close all those dungeons, the brothels of Bangladesh,

Silence the lamenting prostitutes, provide lifelong nutrition,

For Africa's diseased and dying multitudes,

Do not arrows pierce our hearts, bodies and minds?

Do we not endure the Theban afflictions that Sophocles penned? Then bow down before the king of the universe,

Whose divine beauty kindles all creation,

To raise us all to that imperial state,

Removing the curtains and veils of eternal life.

On Perfection

We must cleanse the stains of pride,

Ego, and arrogance from our personalities,

And quench the fires of anger, hatred, and jealousy from our hearts,

Like a gardener who cuts weeds from a spring-time garden,

Only then will we become the elect of God,

And be among his beloved.

On Life

We never chose to enter this world,

And we mourn our exit,

The sunrise of life is destined

For the sunset of decrepit age,

To endure all the arrows that strike our hearts,

Shafts that pierce the body and afflict the mind,

How long do the peaks of happiness last?

Progenitor of our heavens and hells,

Grant us health and happiness like a thousand cocktails
of milk and honey,

Nikki, the memory of our ancient romance,

Brings lasting perfume to my heart,

And makes me forget all painful episodes.

Prayer (1)

Keep us steadfast in our faith in you,

In our periods of hell, and periods of paradise,

In hopes, desires, and dreams , that fail,

Into the abyss of disappointment and despair,

Lift us from the vortex of our pain,

Of the arrows that strike our hearts, bodies, and minds,

How long do the peaks of happiness last?

Heal us with your all healing rays, you, light of the cosmos,

Remove the fires of anger, hatred, and jealousy from our hearts,

With the cool showers of monsoon rains,

Even if our life in this world is profitless and futile,

Grant us the boundless paradise of eternity.

Prayer (2)

Lord, your chosen, beloved, and elect are suffering,

From fatal arrows in their hearts, bodies, and minds,

Of hopes, dreams, and desires that fail,

That vanish like mirages in a wasteland,

Of difficulties, tragedies, and hardships,

Grant us medicine for our hearts, bodies, and minds,

You all healing physician,

Convert the poison of our hearts into honey,

Make the prison-house of this world,

A haven of comfort, luxury, felicity, and health,

Place the fragrant garlands of faith in our hearts,

Our lifelong relationship with you, our lord.

On Despair

What are hopes, desires, and dreams that never become reality?

They are like weary wanderers in deserts, deceived by mirages,

Lord, set all my hopes for the hereafter,

My thirsty life for your eternal oasis,

Everlasting fountains of happiness,

Many populations live in poverty, oppression, and war zones,

The lamentations and cries of Gaza, Kashmir, and Palestine,

The diseased, dying, and starving multitudes of Africa,

If desires had wings, they would soar like eagles above the misty clouds,

Far, far, above the fetters and chains of earthly circumstances.

A Prayer for Improvement

We must remove from our hearts the fires,

Of anger hatred and jealousy,

And fetter our mouths and chain our actions,

When we are under their spell.

We must remove from our personalities,

The stains of ego, pride, and arrogance,

Like a gardener who plucks weeds from a flowery garden,

Only then will we be among god's chosen, beloved, and elect.

Lyrical Poems

There is a romance diviner than life,

That the throbbing heart cannot fathom,

Like a lovely glimpse of a distant future,

Removing the curtains and veils of eternal life,

The mortal heart is raised to more sublime latitude,

Like the pearly crests of the lofty stars,

And this brief odyssey of flesh forgotten,

So she raised me to this imperial state,

And I forgot all the common arrows of life,

And tasted all the crystalline floods,

That are often denied to this posterity.

Look beloved, upon the moonlit lake,

How goddess Cynthia shines upon the shimmering waters,

How the roof of heaven is adorned

With the beaming moon and stars,

Heavenly choirs are singing their hymns,

Accompanied by flying glow-worms,

This, goddess, lofty and pure,

Is the gift and trophy to our favoured life,

Look how the pearl multitudes of the stars,

And apollos throne upon the auroras,

Collaborate like the portents of supremist felicity,

These lush bastions of ageless floras,

That survive the centuries, are evergreen in winters,

Our youthful visages at full meridian,

Where time writes no wrinkles or decays,

Therefore, we are most blessed and fortunate,

That we depend not upon a fictitious paradise,

But it is incarnated in our mortal day.

On Beauties

We abhor the sacrilegious and profane inventions of
time,

Yet elevate and enthrone these messiah-like beauties,

Moulded and painted by divinity,

The imperishable candles of felicity alight.

On the Nature of Life

We never choose to enter this world,

We are often afflicted with knives in our hearts,

Arrows in our bodies, and tempests in our minds,

We all experience periods of heaven and hell,

Like a swinging pendulum,

How long do the peaks of happiness last?

Lord, grant us lasting happiness and health,

Like a thousand cocktails of milk and honey,

Make us governors of our emotions of fire,

Make us monarchs of faith, love, and virtue,

Burning like flames in the niche of our hearts,

Let me exit from this world,

Like doves confined in a cage,

Finally freed into sapphire skies.

Between Paradise or a Prison

Is worldly life a paradise or a prison?

For some a paradise, for some a living hell,

Populations live in poverty, oppression, and war zones,

The injuries and cries of Kashmir and Palestine,

The hunger, thirst, and diseased multitudes of Africa,

We are blessed with a thousand blossoms,

With health and happiness, with rosaries of gratitude,

With the summits of delight,

Show gratitude to God, we are caliphs,

Crowned with sight and hearing, lofty intellects,

If the fires of anger, hatred, and jealousy in our hearts,

Were given freedom in our words and actions,

We become like cyclones, destroying nations, societies
and relationships,

We should be like torches, giving light to candles,

Like fragrant flowers, spreading perfumes of delight,

Like eagles, soaring in the lofty skies.

Faith in God Alone

I bear faith and fealty to God alone,

No false deities or grotesque idolatries,

Of Indian temples, garlanded with stone effigies of Hideous Gods,

No idolatry to beauties with moon white visages,

Or wine-red lips and cheeks,

Or their bodies though they were one of the seven marvels of the world

futile to me are embellished palaces,

Hoarded wealth or Persian concubines,

I sustained the dynasty of faith, love, and virtue,

Beyond the seven spheres broods the dove Of my mews,

Let my aspiring crescent become the full moon of wisdom Sublime,

My entire life's axle and orbit around God.

Your Beauty

Gift and masterwork of divinity,

Has kept me in vassalage all my life,

Yet I have built a Taj Mahal in verse,

To fortify your memory for all posterity,

Like the immortal fragrance of long faded roses,

Generation after generation shall remember you,

Like the ethereal galleries of midnight stars,

I will raise for your memory, monument divine.

Life and Art

Would that we were those lifeless mosaics,

Or the legendary friezes we all admire,

Liberated from flesh, bone, and sinew,

From gethsemane, injuries, and afflictions,

Plague the entrails of our living anatomies,

We suffer like the destructions of troy,

And the ban afflictions assault us,

Pining for those Hellenic masterworks,

Longing to merge in them forever.

On Emotional Pain

Emotional pain hurts more than the wounds of the body,

Of life that throws spears at us, and warfare in relationships,

Of tragedies that scar us forever,

Without sickness and injury,

We can never enjoy health and healing,

Pain makes the taste of happiness sweeter,

Without the barren snow of winter,

We would never long for the temperate rose gardens of spring

On Great Poets

They seek not the praises and accolades of posterity,

They are intoxicated by springtime's lovely incarnations,

The regal banquets of scriptures, philosophy and knowledge,

They give radiance to life's charnels and tombs,

With poetry whose ambitious steeds outpace,

All the common flights of posterity,

They provide refreshing springs for thirsty existences,

And cancel the brackish and polluted rivers where many drink,

They provide sweet honey and manna,

For the starving multitudes of humanity.

The Jail

I yearn to escape from the jail of the world,

The prison of the body,

Like a fluttering falcon finally freed of its cage of steel,

Or a diseased eagle perishing in the scorching Sahara,

Looking at envy at the azure vault of the sky,

If all my hopes and dreams are delusions, lord,

This brief term an anguished prison sentence,

O opener of the bars, free me into the gorgeous meadows of immortality.

Perfection

We must quench the fires of anger, hatred and jealousy from our hearts,

And remove the stains of ego and arrogance from our personalities,

Like a gardener who cuts weeds from a flowery garden,

Only then will we be among god's chosen, beloved, and elect,

Like a few shining stars in a dark sky.

Prayer from the Heart

Lord, nullify all these molten combustions,

Bestow upon me the opium of true faith,

My life pious as the lovely lilacs of May,

Calm the tides of this sulphur filled strife,

Grant me the highest crown of virtues,

Fill these dark entrails with heavenly perfumes,

Give me shield against life's arrows,

Till I live convinced of my salvation.

Her Exit

Her exit from my life was the apocalypse of my
happiness,

Her affections were more intoxicating than a thousand
glasses of wine,

She was fairer than a lily that blossoms in May,

She was the candle of hope in my darkest hours,

I believe not in the profane operations of stars,

For they are not despotic senators,

To execute and crucify our mortal lives,

I desire Lethean forgetfulness of mortality,

To forget this brief pilgrimage of flesh,

Her memory is fresh as vernal meadows,

Yet sullen mists like a black cloak,

Cover all of the budding infant floras

Like towering arcades with illustrious frescoes,

Resist all the linear tragedies of time,

In their frozen utopias forever adorned,

I wish we were like those byzantine mosaics,

Of saints and patriarchs in their fleshless paradise,

Having conquered the plague of flesh,

Shall I not like Columbus seek fresher shores?

A Tribute

Her beauty is like the full moon on the darkest midnight,

Her beauty is like the gorgeous meadows of June,

Her love is more priceless than mountains of gold and silver,

Her biography is free from the arrows of suffering,

She is a solitary star in a black sky,

She is like a jewel amid heaps of trash,

Her beauty is matchless her charms peerless,

When I am thirsty, she gives me fresh fountains,

She is a shining beacon that guides me towards light.

Love is a Queen

Love is the queen of all virtues,

She often flaunts her golden torch,

And then the flame is quenched forever,

Like the amorous heat of Helen and Paris joined,

Cancelled by the zodiacs and prey to the apocalypse,

I have purchased a sweeter paradise,

More pristine than Cordelia's affections,

And the stars fling no archeries upon my hallowed life,

The periods of dungeons I have outlived,

The image of my beloved like a fresh sunrise,

Awakens me from the coma of my dreams,

Like the choiring larks at morns heraldry,

Kiss good night to midnights ethiop canopy,

She waits for me somewhere, and till we meet,

I wish snail paced time would run a marathon.

Goddess of Beauty

Goddess of beauty, too divine for the world,

Unaccustomed to travail, and untutored in eclipse,

To tread the thorns and foot bleeding briars of life,

Consigned to this fallen, fallen, globe,

The seal and obituary of your divinity,

Let your wisdoms torch brighten all dungeons and charnels,

Like, when golden robed dawn, dressed in regality,

Kisses the floras to life and fragrance,

These autocracies of the highest blisses,

That perish in the grave's immortal glooms,

Virgin heavenly and divine,

Rose lipped and blushing cheeks,

And complexion fairer than many full moons,

May never your meridian glory

Decline like the withered lilies of winter.

On the Life of this World

Why should I love the life of this world?

A brief flame that expires, a blink of an eye,

A swinging pendulum between happiness and pain,

The peaks of happiness have descents,

Lord, make my eclipsed periods into fresh mornings,

Give me falcon flights into skies of delight

Why should I form a relationship with humanity?

Of life that flings spears at us,

Hurling scimitars in our hearts and bodies,

Brewing tempests in our minds,

And warfare in relationships,

Those dearest to us exit from this world forever,

Those closer to us than our hearts throbbing's,

Leaving forever vanished presences,

From whence rivers of tears flow endlessly,

Worldly life is a fleeting span, seek instead,

The eternal palace of felicity,

To quench the fires of anger, hatred, and jealousy,

By bathing in gods refreshing fountains,

To gain the peaks of virtues, qualities of love,

To become billionaires in righteous deeds,

To rear impregnable faith like a mountain of granite,

These are festive drums and distant clarions,

Chants and calls towards the limitless ocean of eternal paradise.

On her Love

She became the sunrise, orient, and dawn of my life,

After an era of a long eclipse,

She was whiter than a Lilly flower of May,

Her love was like a garden in the scorching Sahara,

Her beauty was like a violet garden that blossoms in winter,

She was an undying candle of hope in my midnight,

She was the messiah of my life gethsemane,

She became the elixir of my life,

The sustaining morphine for my wounds,

Like a wingless eagle perishing in the desert,

I was furnished with pinions,

And my flight soared beyond the blue hemispheres.

My existence

Why isn't my existence like the stars?

That endure forever and never fade,

Or pure and virtuous as the virginal skies,

Shining with the pristine glow of many gems,

I seek a summit beyond the reach of posterity,

Yet i must endure the ruthless decrees of time,

Like a victim pawn,

Yet my life is sponsored by the divine,

That make my virtues like those imperishable fires

Lord, grant me the nectars of the divine happiness

Of true love, the chalice of wine intoxicating and lasting,

Like the sun nourishes the infant floras,

Make my blossom timeless

God, you cause the sun to rise and set,

By your decree, a thousand rose gardens blossom,

Heal the injuries done to my heart and the decades of my life,

Light my heart with a lamp of inner peace,

By your miracle and your written decree,

Make all my hopes and dreams into a manifest reality.

The Comfort of Death

Disturb not with footsteps, the silent and gothic cemetery,

With lamenting yew trees shading the consecrated spot,

The corpses to dust in the black depth of the grave,

And the sweet and nectar filled slumbers of death,

Death, the beloved of multitudes, the sufferings of life over,

How the stars shine, the zodiacal signs appear,

To predict to mortals how brief their lives flames are,

To remind them of their mortality, to purify their hearts and personalities,

From the chaff, the rotten harvest of sin and iniquity,

Though pearls from abysmal oceans are rare,

She is a pearl i have discovered from a hidden oyster,

The blessed trinity of beauty, virtues, and wisdom,

And though our union is destined to be deaths prey,

And centuries and eons will devour the skeleton of her heavenly frame,

In the boundless realm of paradise,

We shall share a mutual immortality.

Weary Pilgrims

We are like weary pilgrims struggling against the scorching siroccos,

Like athletes desiring to raise trophies,

A mountaineer seeking a summit should never surrender halfway,

Yet mountaineers who conquer summits desire higher summits,

If we cross oceans, we quest for ocean after ocean, coast after coast,

Become like archers whose arrows hit targets,

Become footballers who kick into goals,

Dreamers whose dreams become realities,

To achieve the supreme felicity of life,

On the journey of life, never stop, keep on walking.